MILLIE BOBBY BROWN

ACTRESS & MODEL

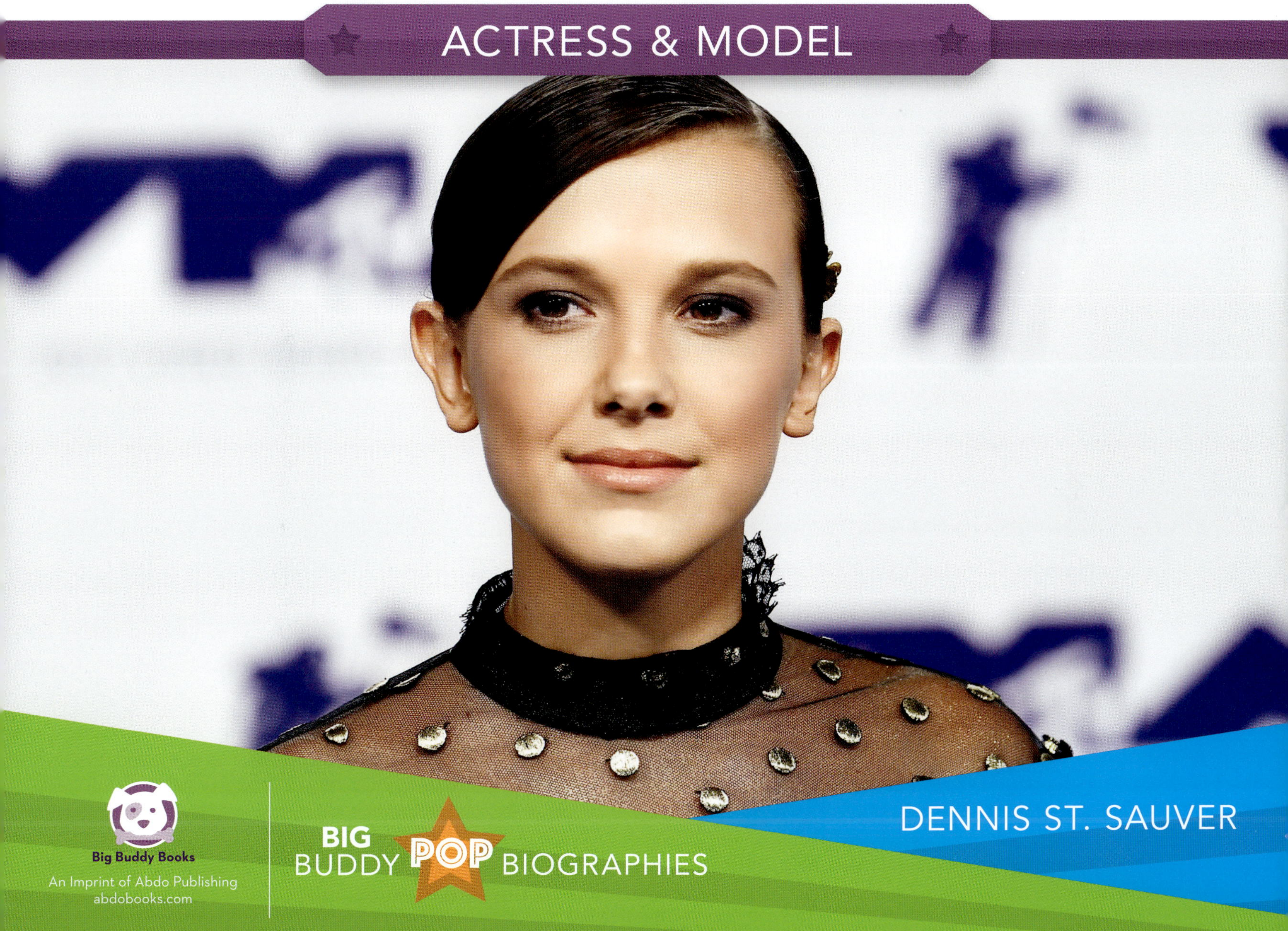

DENNIS ST. SAUVER

Big Buddy Books
An Imprint of Abdo Publishing
abdobooks.com

BIG BUDDY POP BIOGRAPHIES

abdobooks.com

Published by Abdo Publishing, a division of ABDO, PO Box 398166, Minneapolis, Minnesota 55439.

Printed in the United States of America, North Mankato, Minnesota.
102018
012019

Cover Photo: Frazer Harrison/Getty Images.
Interior Photos: Alberto E. Rodriguez/Getty Images (pp. 23, 25); Charley Gallay/Getty Images (p. 15); Dimitrios Kambouris/Getty Images (p. 21); Frazer Harrison/Getty Images (p. 11); Frederick M. Brown/Getty Images (p. 9); Handout/Getty Images (p. 17); John Phillips/Getty Images (p. 5); Kevin Winter/Getty Images (pp. 27, 29); Theo Wargo/Getty Images (p. 13); Vittorio Zunino Celotto/Getty Images (p. 19).

Coordinating Series Editor: Tamara L. Britton
Contributing Series Editor: Jill M. Roesler
Graphic Design: Jenny Christensen, Cody Laberda

Library of Congress Control Number: 2018948437

Publisher's Cataloging-in-Publication Data

Names: St. Sauver, Dennis, author.
Title: Millie Bobby Brown / by Dennis St. Sauver.
Description: Minneapolis, Minnesota : Abdo Publishing, 2019 | Series: Big buddy pop biographies set 4 | Includes online resources and index.
Identifiers: ISBN 9781532117978 (lib. bdg.) | ISBN 9781532171017 (ebook)
Subjects: LCSH: Brown, Millie Bobby, 2004- --Juvenile literature. | Actors--United States--Biography--Juvenile literature. | Television actors and actresses--Biography--Juvenile literature. | Fashion models--Biography--Juvenile literature.
Classification: DDC 791.45028092 [B]--dc23

CONTENTS

ACTRESS AND MODEL

Millie Bobby Brown is an English actress and model. She got her start as an actress on the TV **series** *Once Upon a Time in Wonderland*. And she began her modeling **career** when she was 11 years old.

SNAPSHOT

NAME:
Millie Bobby Brown

BIRTHDAY:
February 19, 2004

BIRTHPLACE:
Málaga, Spain

TELEVISION SHOWS:
Stranger Things, *Once Upon a Time in Wonderland*

FAMILY TIES

Millie was born on February 19, 2004, in Málaga, Spain. Her parents are Kelly and Robert Brown. She has two sisters and a brother. Millie's family is originally from the **UK**. When she was eight years old, they moved to Orlando, Florida.

DID YOU KNOW?

Millie is deaf in one ear. But it has not slowed her acting and modeling careers.

WHERE IN THE WORLD?

BAY OF BISCAY
FRANCE
BALEARIC SEA
Portugal
SPAIN
BALEARIC ISLANDS
Málaga
ATLANTIC OCEAN
MEDITERRANEAN SEA
Algeria
Morocco

N
W
E
S

EARLY YEARS

In Orlando, Millie began taking acting classes. That is when a **talent scout** from Hollywood, California, discovered her acting skills.

The scout told Millie's parents to move to Hollywood where Millie could **audition**. There, she got the **role** of young Alice in *Once Upon a Time in Wonderland*.

After just one audition, Millie got the part of Madison in BBC America's TV show *Intruders*.

GROWING UP

The star's **career** continued to grow. In 2014, she starred in the TV **series** *Intruders*. Later, she appeared in other popular shows such as *Modern Family* and *Grey's Anatomy*.

One of Millie's good friends is dancer and actress Maddie Ziegler *(right)*.

Millie is extremely popular on **social media**. On Instagram, she has more than 16 million followers!

Fans also like to see Millie in **interviews**. She has appeared on *The Tonight Show Starring Jimmy Fallon*. She also went on *The Late Show with Stephen Colbert*.

The young actress can also rap! She rapped about *Stranger Things* on *The Tonight Show Starring Jimmy Fallon*.

BIG BREAK

In 2016, Millie began playing the **role** of Eleven in *Stranger Things*. She got to act alongside world-famous actress Winona Ryder. She also became friends with **co-stars** Finn Wolfhard and Noah Schnapp.

Millie and co-star Noah Schnapp *(right)* liked to trick each other on set!

Millie appeared in a music video for the singer Sigma in 2016. One year later, she was in another music video for the band The xx.

In 2018, Millie appeared in a Maroon 5 video for the song "Girls Like You." She worked with stars like Ellen DeGeneres, Gal Gadot, and Cardi B.

DID YOU KNOW?

Millie enjoys spending time with her family. On Sundays, they have dinner and watch films at home.

Millie went on a family vacation to Disney's Magic Kingdom Park in 2016.

FASHION MODEL

The talented actress is also an up-and-coming model. In 2017, Millie became a model for the Calvin Klein brand.

At the time, Millie was only 12 years old. She was the youngest model to be at the center of a Calvin Klein campaign.

Millie has to get her mother's approval on the clothes she models.

Later in 2017, she signed with the **agency** IMG Models. That same year, she was on the cover of *InStyle* magazine. She appeared upside-down while wearing a pink gown!

In 2018, the model attended a fashion show in Milan, Italy. She was also seen at New York Fashion Week in New York City.

DID YOU KNOW?

Millie loves orca whales and dolphins.

When she was 14, Millie was named one of *Time* magazine's 100 Most Influential People of 2018. She was the youngest person to ever receive that honor.

STRANGER THINGS

Stranger Things is a **thriller** that plays on Netflix. Millie had to shave her head for the **role** of Eleven. But that did not bother her. She wanted to be a serious actor. And she knew her hair would grow back soon.

Millie wore sneakers to the Screen Actors Guild (SAG) Awards so she could dance at the after parties.

AWARDS

When she was 12, Millie was **nominated** for a SAG **Award**. The award was for an Outstanding **Performance** by a Female Actor. She has been a winner or nominee for 21 different awards.

In 2017, she won the MTV Movie and TV Award for Best Actor in a Show. The next year, she earned the Kids' Choice Award for Favorite TV Actress.

Millie and her *Stranger Things* co-stars took home a 2017 SAG Award!

GIVING BACK

Millie spends her free time doing **charity** work. In 2017, she joined UNICEF to talk about World Children's Day. She raised money to help children across the world.

The next year, she helped raise $40,000 for the Olivia Hope **Foundation**. This cause fights against a medical condition called cancer.

Millie wore a special jacket to the 2018 Kids' Choice Awards. The jacket had the names of all those who died at the Parkland School in Florida.

BUZZ

Millie continues to work hard on the set of *Stranger Things*. In 2019, she will also appear in the film *Godzilla: King of the Monsters*. Fans are excited to see what else Millie does next!

DID YOU KNOW?

In June 2018, Millie broke her kneecap. Sadly, she had to miss the MTV Movie and TV Awards because of it.

Millie is a fan of singers Adele and Amy Winehouse. But her favorite singer is Ed Sheeran.

GLOSSARY

agency a business that provides a particular service.

audition (aw-DIH-shuhn) to give a trial performance showcasing personal talent as a musician, a singer, a dancer, or an actor.

award something that is given in recognition of good work or a good act.

career a period of time spent in a certain job.

charity a group or a fund that helps people in need.

co-star one of two or more main performers who star in a movie or play.

foundation (faun-DAY-shuhn) an organization that controls gifts of money and services.

interview a meeting at which people talk to each other in order to ask questions and get information.

nominate to name as a possible winner.

performance an activity that a person or group does to entertain an audience.

role a part an actor plays.

series a set of similar things or events in order.

social media a form of communication on the Internet where people can share information, messages, and videos. It may include blogs and online groups.

talent scout a person whose job is to find talented performers or athletes.

thriller a story full of exciting action, mystery, adventure, or suspense.

UK the united countries of England, Scotland, Wales, and Northern Ireland.

ONLINE RESOURCES

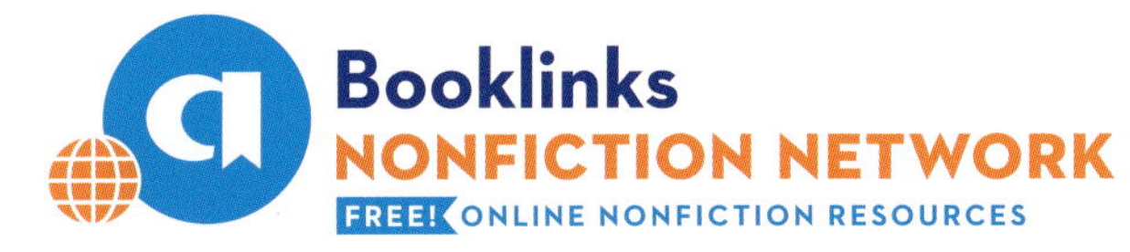

To learn more about Millie Bobby Brown, visit **abdobooklinks.com**. These links are routinely monitored and updated to provide the most current information available.

INDEX